A Green River
in Spring

Author Photo: Lillian Koo
Cover Photo: *Map of West Lake, Hangzhou, China*. Image from Wikipedia Comm█
Cover and text design by Katherine Wintersteen
Titles and text set in Old Style and Bodoni

Printed on acid-free paper.

Coal Hill Review is an imprint of Autumn House Press, a nonprofit
corporation with the mission of publishing and promoting poetry
and other fine literature.

Autumn House Press Staff
Editor-in-Chief: Michael Simms
Managing Editor: Giuliana Certo
Associate Editor: Christine Stroud
Assistant Editor: Alison Taverna
Intern: Ashleigh Fox

Autumn House Press receives state arts funding support
through a grant from the Pennsylvania Council on the Arts,
a state agency funded by the Commonwealth of Pennsylvania,
and the National Endowment for the Arts, a federal agency.

ISBN: 978-1-938769-05-4

A Green River in Spring

Poems by
Matthew Thorburn

Coal Hill Review
Pittsburgh, Pennsylvania

CONTENTS

—for Lillian
and for Preston

First Light

The sun breaks like an egg over everything
east of here. *Stop stop, enough enough,*
the sparrows say—or that's what Lao Wen says

they say in Chinese. Take your tarnished
horn, your wooden flute and break
this silence—alone beside the dark water, desperate

for the birds to get to work—delicate
as the last skin of ice on a winter river's wrist.

Birds Before Winter

Dabbing lather across my chin, I picture you: bent low
over the tap, drinking from your cupped hands.

You probably aren't even up yet. Hair a tangle
on the covers, eyelids made pale by the sun.

Sweeping the back step I find a cricket,
wings laced with frost. The leaves keep falling.

I look for you in all the things that are not you.
The plate of milk, left by the cat, sours.

You must be filling the red teapot
with water now, measuring green tea.

The birds wing their way south. They take
the sky with them, each black scrap.

A Lishan Bell

Old hermit like a crane
nesting high in the mountains—

is he a sage? Is he lonely?
In his hut he hides

a painting of Xian
within its ancient city walls.

If a bell has no clapper
strike it with a log.

Even There

All day you sit by the river—
a train arrives, a train leaves
and all day the river pushes on,

never all getting there.
Better to be this tiny brown bird
stopping to peck at something

that you can't see, that—
you look away, you look back—
probably isn't even there.

October in Xihu

The last yellow leaves
creak and moan
        as the wind sweeps through—

a swan
circles the slate-gray lake,
        searching for her mate.

Snow Falls All Night

Judge a horse by the sharpness
of his ears, Lao Wen says.
Judge a man by how often
he sharpens his knife. Snow falls

all night and erases these words.
A knife shines on the table.
No sound now but the horse
stamping once more in his stall.

A Blessing

Whether it was your sister or your girlfriend
doesn't matter. We got her.

I am writing this to say peanut butter
makes great bait. Dear mouse

behind my bookshelf, a cockroach can live
for nine days without its head

before it starves to death.
May you be so lucky.

At White Horse Temple

Slip off your shoes to enter the temple.
But what if—

          So you ask me to let go
of worldly things and so I do

until what slips into my mind
is a skinny boy hotfooting it
down the alley, laughing, skidding

around a corner, pausing now
before a bright shop window
to look down and admire my shoes.

An Anhui Well

Once a boy slipped
down a well in far
Anhui. He surfaced deep
in Mongolia, whispering
through his fever
of the vast, star-clotted sky

he swam beneath.
Once I called down
into that dark glitter—
then cursed, then bargained,
then begged—until
someone else called back.

What Waits for Us

My neighbor's window throws a stripe
of light across the grass:

a line tossed out to anyone—

you? me?—still up at this hour, still
wandering, still wondering

what waits for us in the dark.

Autumn

Not the moonlit gravel path
but the cool air caught
inside a stone for a thousand years.

Before the First Black Horse

White is the color of the spirit world, so offer peaches, offer chestnuts to your ancestors, your elders. White of sugar, white of salt, the river churning white in its rapids. Color of death forgetting, of snow drifting down like the sheets that cover each table and chair, each tall dim mirror in Lao Wen's darkened house. *White snow in early spring,* Xiao Ming and I sing, *falling, falling everywhere,* as we tramp through the woods. That's how it goes, that old Mongolian horse trader's song. But isn't it always white as it falls, always white against the bare trees before the first black horse rushes through?

Sunday Morning

the sleeve of my breath hangs in the air

    on a park bench four sparrows sit in a row

more trees than people in Lishan Square

    the statue of Mao wears a toupee of snow

A Branch

falls into
the river and a bird
alights there

and now we
stand here, you and I,
and watch—

gray branch, brown
river, a speck
of pale blue—

how quickly
this slips away.

A Green River in Spring

Taoists hitch a ride on a crane
to get to heaven, or else
become cranes themselves.
Better than wishing yourself
governor of Hangzhou next time
around, or a rich man who pays

someone else to mind his farm
and winds up broke.
Just don't get confused
and return as a stork—
they can't sing, can't even talk.
Yes, slip away, get going,
disappear into the mountains
or the cold whisper

of a green river in spring.
I would, I would,
though knowing me
I'll probably just come back
like your gray cat—
scooching across the floor
inch by inch all afternoon
to stay inside this
yellow square of light.

Water Rises Once More

Sipping dew to stretch out your life?
Emperor Wu tried that trick
and you know where to find him.
Meanwhile the Huai River still floods
each spring. Nothing wrong

with growing *old*—it sounds
like *Chrysanthemum* in Chinese
or used to, long ago. The water rises
once more. Watch the yellow petals
float up in your chipped cup
as you wait for your tea to cool.

At the New Year Festival

The monk wearing a paper mask stoops down
to peer at the boy wearing a paper mask staring up.

Cicada

Where do the bees go in winter,
their hives shuttered in ice?
When spring rains tear down
the spider's web, she strings up
another. It seems the same
cicadas sing in the willow leaves
each year. In spring they rise

from the dirt. When Lao Wen
died, great-grandmother placed
a jade cicada on his tongue.
You are my salt, she said
though she was already alone—

angry and alone beside
dark Lake Tai. East wind
blows, swallows come home.
Now he will stay at Lake Tai
forever. Blackened by fire
the cicada slips into her pocket:
still warm, starting to sing.

Song

Sky of finger-smudged glass. Spikes
of wild asparagus in the wet ditch at the side of the road.
Someone roll out the piano, please,

the old upright in need of a tune-up. Now the yellow
elbow of the river in what's left
of the light. The river that remembers

and forgets, that one. A bright blade of light glances off
the trees; the trees
glance back. Give me the grace of distance

and if possible
a pearl-gray moon masked with a bit of cloud.

The Other Side

In the old ink
and brush style of painting
the brush can't leave
the paper until
you're done so that it's all
one long line
that turns and turns and
loops back, taking
its time, and sometimes

standing here outside the door
as snow filters
across the blue-black sky
and I can hear you
on the other side
I can't remember
if I've only just arrived
or it's time for me to go.

ACKNOWLEDGMENTS

Thank you to the editors and readers of the journals where some of these poems first appeared over the years, often in earlier versions:

32 Poems Magazine: "A Blessing"

The American Poetry Review: "A Lishan Bell," "At White Horse Temple," "Autumn," "The Other Side"

Cumberland River Review: "First Light"

Lilliput Review: "October in Xihu"

The MacGuffin: "Birds Before Winter"

Margie: The American Journal of Poetry: "Sunday Morning"

Tiferet: "Song"

"A Blessing" was also included in *Bigger Than They Appear: An Anthology of Very Short Poems* (Accents Publishing, 2011), edited by Katerina Stoykova-Klemer.

The first spark for many of these poems came from reading classical Chinese and Japanese poetry. I'm grateful to the translators whose work makes those poems available to me, especially Red Pine, David Hinton, Kenneth Rexroth, Robert Hass, and G.W. Robinson. I also wish to thank my mother-in-law, Mrs. Fong Koo, for sharing her love of Chinese poetry and for our many conversations about reading poems in translation. And special thanks once more to Stuart Greenhouse and Jay Leeming, my old friends in poetry, for their encouragement and thoughtful advice.

ABOUT THE AUTHOR

Matthew Thorburn is the author of three books
of poems, *This Time Tomorrow, Every Possible
Blue,* and *Subject to Change,* and an earlier
chapbook, the long poem *Disappears in the Rain.*
He lives with his wife and son in New York City,
where he works as the communications manager
for an international law firm.

The *Coal Hill Review* Chapbook Series

Winner of the 2014 Prize
A Green River in Spring
Matthew Thorburn

Winner of the 2013 Prize
The Welter of Me & You
Peter Schireson

Co-winner of the 2012 Prize
Prayers of an American Wife
Victoria Kelly

Co-winner of the 2012 Prize
Rooms of the Living
Paul Martin

A Special Edition
Irish Coffee
Jay Carson

Winner of the 2011 Prize
Bathhouse Betty
Matt Terhune

A Special Edition
Crossing Laurel Run
Maxwell King

Winner of the 2010 Prize
Shelter
Gigi Marks

Winner of the 2009 Prize
Shake It and It Snows
Gailmarie Pahmeier

Winner of the 2008 Prize
The Ghetto Exorcist
James Tyner